go figure

Use your mathematical skills to explore the exciting world of extreme sports, and solve puzzles along the way to turn you into an ace sports reporter.

LEARN ABOUT IT
RATIOS

)GO FIGURE!

This section will take you through the mathematical ideas you'll need to complete each mission.

The practical examples in this section will test your knowledge of the ideas you've just learnt.

ANSWERS AND GLOSSARY

Answers to the Go Figure! challenges can be found on page 28. Words in *italics* appear in the glossary on page 30.

You might find some of the questions in this book are too hard to do without the help of a calculator. Ask your teacher about when and how to use a calculator.

WHAT EQUIPMENT DO YOU NEED?

Pen or pencil

Notepad

Protractor

SKYRUNNING

Your first mission will take you up some of the world's highest mountains to try skyrunning. This extreme sport involves running races against other competitors at altitudes of more than 2000 metres, adding up your scores as you go.

LEARN ABOUT IT
MENTAL ADDITION

There are lots of strategies for adding lists of numbers in your head. Have you tried these?

Look for numbers that join to make 10 or a *multiple* of 10, like 7 + 3, 36 + 14, 88 + 12 and so on.

36 + 38 + 34 + 32 + 30 = 70 + 70 + 30 = 170.

Another strategy is to add the tens and the units separately, which is particularly useful if the units digits are small. To add 40, 42, 31, 62 and 51, add 40, 40, 30, 60 and 50 which is 220, and then add on 2, 1, 2 and 1 to give the total 226.

If the numbers are quite close to each other, use multiplication. To add 44, 46, 44, 46 and 48 you could think of them each as the number 44 and multiply 44 by 5, which is 40 x 5 = 200 plus 4 x 5 = 20 = 220. Then add the differences between the numbers and 44, which is 2, 2 and 4 = 8. The total altogether is 228.

Round numbers to the **nearest 10** and then make adjustments afterwards. Start by writing how much larger or smaller each number is than its nearest multiple of 10:

88 is 2 less than 90 which we can write as -2
61 is 1 more than 60 which we can write as +1

To add 34, 88, 61, 27 and 59, add 30, 90, 60, 30 and 60 = 270
then adjust +4, -2, +1, -3, -1 to give the answer 269.

〉GO FIGURE!

In each skyrunning season, competitors enter at least five races and are given points according to where they finish: 100 points go to the winner, 88 for second place, 78 for third place, down to two points for 40th place. The best four results across the season are added up, and the runner with the highest total is the champion.

RACE	COMPETITOR					
	Sam	Jo	Francis	Ali	Alex	Jamie
Race 1 Spain, May 25	88	78	66	100	2	20
Race 2 Italy, June 21	78	100	66	42	88	64
Race 3 Switzerland, August 10	64	54	64	6	78	4
Race 4 Switzerland, August 28	88	38	62	74	100	78
Race 5 Italy, October 10	78	100	68	64	88	82

1. Work out the total of Francis's five scores altogether. Use one of the mental strategies suggested.

2. Now work out the total of Jamie's five scores. Who scored most points in the five races altogether, Francis or Jamie?

3. For each competitor write which is their lowest/worst score.

4. **Taking only their best four scores, and ignoring the worst score, find the total for each competitor.**

5. Which of the competitors should be crowned the champion (with the highest score)?

SKELETON

Now you must find out about the skeleton. In this dangerous sport, you travel on a special tray without brakes at very high speeds along an ice track. Your nose is just centimetres from the ground!

LEARN ABOUT IT
DECIMALS

Decimals are another way of writing fractions.

	fraction		decimal
			units . tenths hundredths
two hundredths	$\frac{2}{100}$		0 . 0 2
one tenth	$\frac{1}{10}$		0 . 1
14 hundredths	$\frac{14}{100}$		0 . 1 4
113 hundredths	$\frac{113}{100}$		1 . 1 3

When comparing decimals, remember that the columns to the right become smaller and smaller so start by comparing the left-hand columns. The column to the right of the hundredths column is thousandths. One thousandth is one tenth of a hundredth and is very small.

It helps to make sure that the numbers have the same number of digits after the decimal point by writing extra zeros in the positions that have no digit. One tenth or 0.1 is the same as 0.10 – it has 1 tenth and no hundredths. It is easier to see that 0.10 lies between 0.02 and 0.14 than it is to see that 0.1 lies between them. So, to order 1.3, 1.25 and 1.287, change them to 1.300, 1.250 and 1.287. It's then easy to see that 1.300 is the largest number and 1.250 is the smallest number.

〉GO FIGURE!

There are only a few official skeleton ice tracks around the world. They have varying lengths and vertical drops, and have different numbers of curves.

Country	Track	Length (km)	Vertical Drop (m)	Curves
Austria	Igls	1.22	98.1	14
Russia	Paramonovo	1.6	105	19
Russia	Sochi	1.814	131.9	19
Canada	Calgary	1.475	121.48	14
Canada	Whistler	1.45	152	16
Germany	Königssee	1.306	117	13
Germany	Winterberg	1.33	110	14
Germany	Oberhof	1.069	96.37	15
Germany	Altenberg	1.413	122.22	17
United States	Lake Placid	1.455	107	20
United States	Park City	1.34	103.9	15
Switzerland	St Moritz	1.722	130	16
Latvia	Sigulda	1.2	111.5	16
France	La Plagne	1.507	119	19
Japan	Nagano	1.36	113	14
Italy	Cortina d'Ampezzo	1.35	120.45	13
Norway	Lillehammer	1.365	114.3	16

1 Look at the lengths of the first two tracks above. Which is longer? The track named Igls or the one named Paramonovo?

2 Which of the two Canadian tracks
a) has the longer length?
b) has the longer vertical drop?
c) has more curves?

3 Germany has four tracks. Put the tracks in order of length, starting with the longest.

4 Which of all the tracks
a) is the longest?
b) has the greatest vertical drop?
c) has the most curves?

HANG GLIDING

You've been running up mountains and travelling on ice so far. Your next mission is to leave Earth and head up into the air to find out about hang gliding and paragliding. For this you need to know about *ratios*.

Ratios compare two or more things. For example in a tile pattern, for every one black tile there might be eight white tiles, like this:

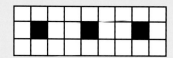

We write the ratio of black to white as **1:8**

08

Ratios can be multiplied or divided to show the same basic relationship. For example, the ratio **1:8** is the same ratio as **2:16**, or **3:24**, or even **100:800**. The ratio **1:8** is the simplest form as it uses the smallest numbers possible.

Triangles whose sides are in the same ratio are called similar triangles. The first triangle on the grid below measures 6 squares across and 2 down.

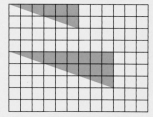

It has the ratio **6:2**. The second triangle is 9 squares across and 3 down and has the ratio **9:3**. These are similar triangles as both can be written as **3:1** in their simplest form.

It is easier to compare ratios when in the form n:1, where n might be a decimal. Divide both numbers in the ratio by the second number.

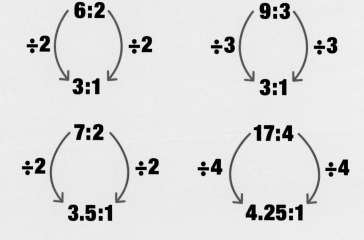

〉GO FIGURE!

Hang gliding and paragliding are described using glide ratios. For instance, gliding 12 m forwards for every 1 m of height lost is the glide ratio 12:1. Paragliders can have glide ratios of up to 10:1 while hang gliders can have ratios of up to 20:1. Compare these ratios to one another to see which are the most impressive.

three paragliding flights

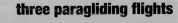

28 m   4 m   18 m   6 m   27 m   3 m

hang gliding flight

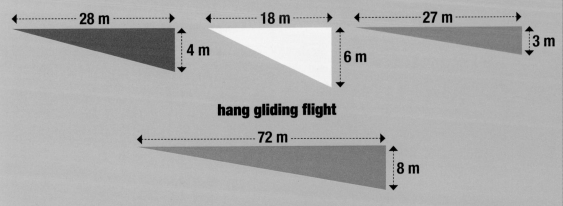

72 m   8 m

1 Above are triangles showing three paragliders' flights. Write each glide ratio in its simplest form.

2 Which of the three paragliding flights has the same glide ratio as the hang gliding flight?

3 Write each of the following ratios in the form n:1.
a) 35 m across for every 5 m down.
b) 15 m across for every 2 m down.
c) 113 m across for every 10 m down.
d) 41 m across for every 4 m down.

4 Which of the ratios in question 3 travels the farthest across for each metre of drop?

WINDSURFING

The extreme sport of windsurfing isn't just about racing across the waves as fast as you can The speed of the wind, your own bodyweight and the size of the sail all affect your performance.

LEARN ABOUT IT AREA

Area **is the amount of surface that something has and it is measured in squares, such as square centimetres (cm²) or square metres (m²).**

10

We can estimate the areas of irregular shapes by counting whole and part squares.
To do this, count the whole squares first, then imagine joining the part squares together to make whole squares to estimate the total. For this sail, we could make an estimate of about 24 squares.

When windsurf sails are made their area is calculated very accurately in metres squared, such as 4 m² or 7.7 m².

⟩GO FIGURE!

This table shows the best sail areas for different windsurfer weights and wind speeds. The sections in yellow are sail sizes that are impractical or not available.

Wind speed in *knots*

Windsurfer weight in kg	10	14	18	22	26	30	34	38
50	6.7	4.8	3.7	3	2.6	2.2	2	1.8
60	8	5.7	4.5	3.7	3.1	2.7	2.4	2.1
70	9.4	6.7	5.2	4.3	3.5	3.1	2.8	2.4
80	10.7	7.7	6	4.9	4.1	3.6	3.2	2.8
90	12.1	8.6	6.7	5.5	4.6	4	3.5	3.2
100	13.4	9.6	7.4	6.1	5.2	4.5	3.9	3.5
110	14.7	10.5	8.2	6.7	5.7	4.9	4.3	3.9

Ideal sail size in m²

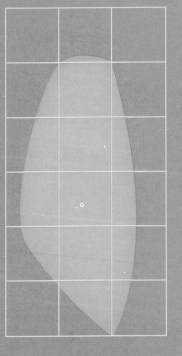

1 Estimate the area of the blue sail on the left, if each square represents 1 m².

2 Given a wind speed of 22 knots, what is the ideal sail size for someone weighing:
a) 50 kg   b) 80 kg   c) 110 kg?

3 James weighs 90 kg. What sail size is ideal for him when the wind speed is:
a) 14 knots b) 26 knots c) 38 knots?

4 A windsurfing club has a sail with an area of 6.7 m². If each of these riders used the sail in the conditions shown, which of these are ideal?

• Sam, who weighs 50 kg, in a wind speed of 18 knots?

• Lucy, who weighs 70 kg, in a wind speed of 14 knots?

• Clive, who weighs 110 kg, in a wind speed of 22 knots?

ICE CLIMBING

Ice climbers use ice axes to haul themselves up giant frozen walls. Vertical or overhanging ice walls are the hardest to climb, while gentler slopes leaning in are easier.

LEARN ABOUT IT

ANGLE AND SCALE DRAWINGS

***Angles* are measured in degrees. There are 90 degrees (90°) in a right angle and 360° in a full turn.**

| 60° | 75° | 90° | 110° |

An angle less than 90° is called an *acute angle*.
Angles between 90° and 180° are called *obtuse angles*.

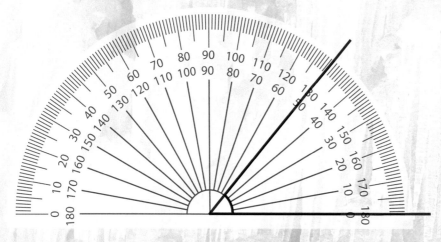

We use a *protractor* to measure and draw angles, lining up the centre of the protractor with the corner of the angle, like this.

Be careful to count around from zero to the line. This line is only 50° not 130°.

When drawing pictures of real-life features, we use a *scale*, such as 1 cm in the picture representing 500 cm in real life. This is written as 1:500. The drawing has the same angles as the feature. Remember that 100 cm = 1m, so 500 cm = 5 m.

⟩GO FIGURE!

Different ice climbs have different grades according to the slope and length of the climb. Look at these scale drawings of different ice walls and decide how difficult each one is.

Climb A
Scale 1:100

Climb B
Scale 1:800

13

....

① Use a protractor to measure the marked angle for each ice climb.

② **Use a ruler to measure the length of each of the lines from the corner of the angle to the highest point in cm.**

③ Use the scales to work out the actual length of each climb in real life.

④ **List the four climbs in order starting with the one you think is easiest, and ending with the hardest climb.**

Climb C
Scale 1:600

Climb D
Scale 1:1000

MOGUL SKIING

Your next extreme sport to research is mogul skiing, which involves skiing down a course that has many mounds and bumps. Judges decide on the score for each skier based on their speed and how they perform the turns and air jumps.

LEARN ABOUT IT
PERCENTAGES

The scores for different skills are given different *percentage* weightings to form a final score.

50 is half of 100, so to find 50 per cent of a number, divide it by 2. To find 25 per cent of a number, divide it by 4.

100%		
50%	25%	25%

To find 10 per cent of a number, divide it by 10.
To find 20 per cent of a number, divide it by 5,
or divide it by 10 and then double the answer.
To find 60 per cent of a number, divide it by 10
and then multiply the answer by 6.

100%		
60%	20%	20%

When finding a *weighted score*, you need to find the given percentage of each score and add the answers together to give a final score. You may find it useful to use a calculator.

⟩GO FIGURE!

The final scores are calculated with the following weightings:

In one competition the scores are rated as follows:
Turns 50% • Air jumps 25% • Speed 25%

100%		
Turns	Air Jumps	Speed

In a second competition they are rated as follows:
Turns 60% • Air jumps 20% • Speed 20%

100%		
Turns	Air Jumps	Speed

1 Kasper scored 30 points in turns, 20 points in air jumps and 12 points in speed. What would his final score be if he was in: a) the first competition b) the second competition?

2 Which weighting suits Kasper best?

3 Kayley scored 20 points in turns, 28 points in air jumps and 13 points in speed. What would her final score be if she was in: a) the first competition b) the second competition?

4 Which weighting suits Kayley best?

MOTOCROSS

Motocross involves riding special motorbikes on rough and bumpy tracks. For your next mission, you need to find out which are the best tyres for this extreme sport.

LEARN ABOUT IT
CIRCLES

This challenge will involve getting to grips with the *radius*, *diameter* and *circumference* of circles.

The radius of a circle is the distance from the edge to the centre of the circle. It is half the length of the diameter which is the widest distance across the circle, through the centre. The circumference is the *perimeter* of the circle – the distance around its edge.

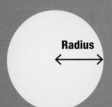

Radius

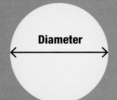

Diameter

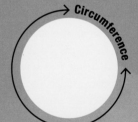

Circumference

There is a special relationship between the diameter of a circle and its circumference. For every circle, the circumference (**c**) is always 3.1412 times the length of the diameter (**d**). We call this number 3.1412 *pi* and write it like this: π.

This gives the *formula* $c = \pi d$

The fraction $^{22}/_{7}$ is sometimes used as an estimate for pi.

If you know how many times a bike tyre has turned along the ground, you can use the circumference to work out how far the bike has travelled. Imagine a spot of paint on the tyre leaving a series of marks on the track.

circumference

⟩GO FIGURE!

Motocross bikes can have different tyre sizes, including having a different front and rear wheel size. The engine drives the back wheel and the wheels rotate at different rates from each other, for example one wheel might make five turns in the same time that the other wheel makes four turns.

- - - - Rim diameter
- - - - Tyre diameter

WHEEL	RIM DIAMETER (WITHOUT THE TYRE)	TYRE DIAMETER
FRONT	40.6 cm	53.2 cm
REAR	35.5 cm	49.0 cm

1 How much larger is: a) the rim diameter of the front wheel than the rear wheel b) the tyre diameter of the front wheel than the rear wheel?

2 Taking π to be 3.14, calculate the circumference of:
a) the front wheel with tyre
b) the rear wheel with tyre.

3 Giving your answer in metres, how far would the motorbike go if: a) the front wheel makes 10 turns while in contact with the ground without slipping b) the rear wheel makes 10 turns while in contact with the ground without slipping?

4 Without leaving the ground or slipping how many times would:
a) the front wheel turn in 585.2 m
b) the rear wheel turn in 585.2 m?

17

CAVING

Cavers, or potholers, explore networks of caves and cracks below ground level. This can involve abseiling, crawling through tight cracks, swimming underwater and rock climbing.

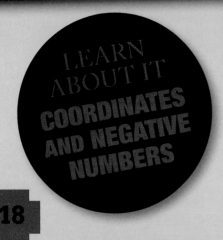

LEARN ABOUT IT

COORDINATES AND NEGATIVE NUMBERS

18

A coordinate grid can be divided into four areas called *quadrants*. The centre of the grid, where the x and y axes cross, is known as the origin.

You can refer to any point by giving its coordinates – these are two numbers in brackets. The first shows the distance you have to go across on the x-axis. The second shows the distance you have to go up or down on the y-axis.

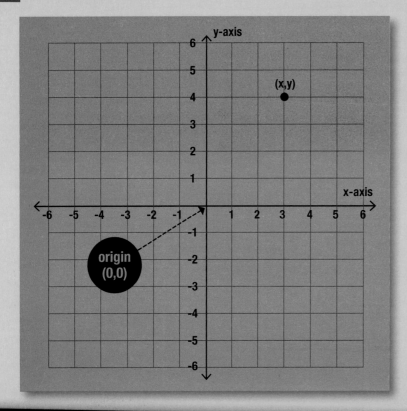

The point (x, y) on the grid to the left is at (3, 4) because, from the origin, you go 3 squares to the right and 4 squares up to reach the point.

All points on the right of the y-axis have positive x values. All points on the left of the y-axis have negative x values. All points above the x-axis have positive y values. All points below the x-axis have negative y values. So (5, -3) is to the right of the y-axis and below the x-axis.

⟩GO FIGURE!

Use your knowledge of *negative numbers* to work out your routes through the cave system.

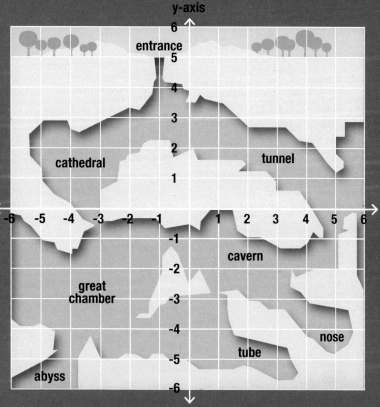

1. Write the coordinates of the entrance to the cave system.

2. **In which part of the cave system are you if you are at:**
   a) (-4, 2)
   b) (-4, -3)
   c) (3, -5)
   d) (5, -4)
   e) (-6, -6)?

3. Follow this route from the entrance, and see where you end up.
   down 2, right 2,
   down 1, right 3,
   down 1, right 1,
   down 3, left 3.

4. **Describe a route to get from (2, -2) to the abyss.**

ABSEILING

Abseiling is a controlled descent down a cliff face or the side of a building using a rope. The rope is secured at the top, and the abseiler carefully descends using a harness that is attached to the rope.

It is possible to find out the height of a tall building or cliff by standing somewhere near its base.

If you know how far from the base you are (**d**) and measure the angle from the ground up to the top of the building (**a**) you can find its height. This method is based on what we know about *right-angled triangles*.

The formula showing how to find the height (**h**) is:

$$h = \tan (a) \times d$$

Tan (which is short for tangent) is found on scientific calculators. It shows the relationship between the angle and two of the sides of a right-angled triangle. If the angle **a** is 30° and the distance, **d**, is 400 m, then we find the height using a calculator by keying in: tan (30) x 400.

The answer is often a long decimal so round it up or down. Rather than writing 230.9401077 m, we could round it to one decimal place: 230.9 m.

h

a

d

❭GO FIGURE!

You visit some different places to abseil from and take lots of measurements. These sketches show the measurements you have taken. Let's see which of the descents is the most challenging!

A

h

40°

d = 500 m

B

h

45°

d = 800 m

C

h

60°

d = 900 m

D

h

35°

d = 600 m

1. Giving each answer to one decimal place, find the height, **h**, for: a) skyscraper A b) skyscraper B c) cliff C d) building D

2. **Which two jumps are a similar height?**

3. What do you notice about **d** and **h** for skyscraper B?

4. **Which of the descents is the: a) largest b) smallest?**

SLACKLINING

Slacklining is similar to tightrope walking but is done on a stretchy line a bit like a very thin trampoline. There are world records for the highest slackline crossing, the longest slackline crossing and data on how quickly lines are crossed.

LEARN ABOUT IT
MEASUREMENT CONVERSIONS

When comparing measurements it is important to know the relationships between units, like this:

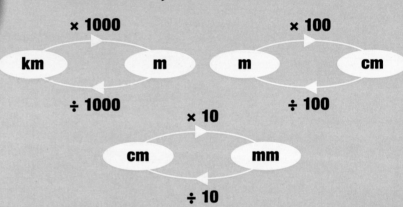

× 1000
km → m
÷ 1000

× 100
m → cm
÷ 100

× 10
cm → mm
÷ 10

Remember to check whether the units of the measurements you are comparing are the same. Here they are all different, but we can change them all to metres by multiplying or dividing by 1000, 100 or 10 using the diagrams above to help us.

6 km	57,300 cm	100,000 mm
x 1000	÷ 100	÷ 10 and then ÷ 100
6000 m	573 m	100 m

Sometimes lengths are given using imperial units. Here are their relationships to other units. Use multiplication and division to convert between them.

Length

1 inch ≈ 2.5 cm
12 inches = 1 foot ≈ 30 cm
3 feet = 1 yard ≈ 90 cm
1760 yards = 1 mile ≈ 1.6 km

≈ means 'approximately equal to'

These are the world slacklining records. They include highlining, which is slacklining over a big drop, and waterlining, which is slacklining over water. Measurements are given in different units.

RECORD	DISTANCE	PERSON	PLACE	DATE
Longest slackline (men)	2000 feet long	Alexander Schulz	Inner Mongolia, China	May 2015
Longest slackline (women)	23,000 cm long	Laetitia Gonnon	Lausanne Switzerland	September 2014
Highest ever slackline	1.2 km high	Andy Lewis	Nevada desert, USA	March 2014
Highest urban highline	185 m high	Reinhard Kleindl	Frankfurt, Germany	May 2013
Longest waterline	363 yards long	Alexander Schulz	Eibsee, Denmark	August 2014
Longest highline (men)	1230 feet long	Alexander Schulz	Yangshuo, China	November 2014
Longest highline (women)	105 m long	Faith Dickey	Moab, USA	November 2014

1 What is the men's longest slackline length: a) in feet b) in centimetres c) in metres?

2 What is the women's longest slackline length: a) in centimetres b) in metres c) in kilometres?

3 How much higher is the highest ever slackline record than the highest urban record, in metres?

4 Convert the longest waterline record into metres.

5 a) Convert the men's longest highline into metres. b) How much more than the women's longest highline record is the men's record, in metres?

23

SNOWBOARDING

For your next mission you must judge halfpipe snowboarding. In a halfpipe competition, snowboarders do tricks down a pipe-shaped course. The scoring system is quite complicated, so make sure you can work out who will win!

LEARN ABOUT IT

MEAN, MEDIAN AND MODE AVERAGES

Averages summarise a set of numbers using just one number. There are different types of averages, including the *mean*, the *median* and the *mode*.

To calculate the mean of a set of numbers, find the total of all the values and then divide it by how many numbers there are.

For example, the **mean** average of 44, 57, 42, 49 and 58 is found by adding them together, then dividing by how many numbers there are, which in this case is 5.

$$44 + 57 + 42 + 49 + 58 = 250$$

$$250 \div 5 = 50$$ The mean of the numbers is 50.

The **median** is found by writing the numbers in order and selecting the middle value. 44, 57, 42, 49 and 58 can be written in order as:

42, 44, 49, 57, 58   The median is the middle value 49.

The **mode** can be used when there is a lot of data and numbers are repeated. The mode is the number that occurs most often in a list of numbers:

3, 6, 3, 5, 6, 4, 6, 3, 4, 3, 4, 6, 7, 3, 3, 3, 5, 3, 7, 8, 2, 3, 7, 1, 3, 5, 3, 6, 6, 7

The mode is 3 as it occurs most often.

❯GO FIGURE!

In halfpipe snowboarding, between three and six judges each give a competitor a maximum of 100 points. If there are six judges the middle four scores are averaged using the mean.

Judges score each rider based on:
- **Flow** – How fluid is the rider in line choice, execution of tricks, landing and movement through the course?
- **Creativity of line** – How well does the rider make creative / artistic use of the halfpipe?
- **Technical difficulty** – How hard are the moves and how well are they being performed?
- **Amplitude** – How high are the tricks?
- **Style** – The hardest to describe, but the most important.

For this competition here are six judges' basic scores, which must be changed into final scores.

NAME	J1	J2	J3	J4	J5	J6	Total of middle four scores	Mean score
Zhang Shi	67	73	75	78	86	70		
Ivan Plotchedov	83	88	86	85	88	94		
David Jenner	91	86	85	93	94	92		
Amru Szalji	86	89	87	88	90	88		
Andreas Schultz	94	95	92	95	98	95		
Kyle Robertson	96	98	96	97	97	95		

1 For each competitor, ignore the highest and lowest of the judges' scores, and find the total of the middle four scores.

2 Divide each total by 4 to find the mean score, giving each as a decimal with 2 decimal places.

3 Write the competitors in order to complete a final winning table. The highest mean score is in first position.

4 Who wins: a) a gold medal
b) a silver medal
c) a bronze medal?

WAKEBOARDING

Wakeboarding involves riding a board over the surface of water. The rider is towed behind a speedboat, typically at speeds of 30–40 km/h (18–25 mph), depending on the board size, the rider's weight, the type of tricks and rider's comfort.

LEARN ABOUT IT
ANGLE AND SPEED

When wakeboarding, your board, hopefully with you on it, can turn.

Angles are measured in degrees, with **90°** in a quarter turn, **180°** in a half turn and **360°** in a full turn.

26

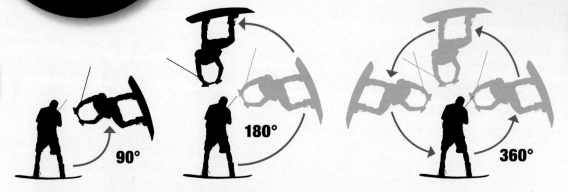

90°   180°   360°

Speeds of fast motorboats are usually measured in kilometres per hour (km/h) or miles per hour (mph). One mile equals about 1.6 km. To approximately convert between units use these formulae:

mph speed × 1.6 = km/h speed   **km/h speed ÷ 1.6 = mph speed**

When working mentally it's easier to use these:

mph speed ÷ 5 × 8 = km/h speed   **km/h speed ÷ 8 × 5 = mph speed**

For example:

35 mph ÷ 5 = 7, 7 × 8 = 56 = 56 km/h

88 km/h ÷ 8 = 11, 11 × 5 = 55 = 55 mph

Use this description of a wakeboarder's ride to answer questions about tricks and speed.

"At the start, the boat was going at an initial speed of 20 mph but sped up to about 40 km/h so I could do some spins. I started with a 'Frontside 360' spin, which is doing a 360° rotation while in the air with my front towards the boat. I then did a 'Backside 540' off the wake where I spin with the back of my body towards the boat first through 540°. I then did a 'Backside 720'. I tried an 'Off-axis 900' spin where my board goes above shoulder level while I do a 900° rotation but haven't perfected it yet. I did a 'Shifty' next, going 90° in one direction and then 90° back in the other. My aim is to do a '1080' spin by doing a 1080° rotation in the air but I'm still working towards it."

27

1 What was the initial speed in km/h?

2 **How many miles per hour did the boat speed up to?**

3 How many quarter turns in: a) the first part of a Shifty b) a Frontside 360?

4 **How many half turns in a: a) Frontside 360 b) Backside 540 c) Backside 720?**

5 Giving fractions in your answers if necessary, write how many full turns there are in a) Backside 540 b) Backside 720 c) Off-axis 900 d) 1080 spin

GO FIGURE! ANSWERS

04–05 Skyrunning
1. 66 + 66 + 64 + 62 + 68 = 326
2. 20 + 64 + 4 + 78 + 82 = 248
Francis scored more points.
3. Sam 64, Jo 38, Francis 62, Ali 6,
Alex 2, Jamie 4
4. Sam 332, Jo 332, Francis 264, Ali 280,
Alex 354, Jamie 244
5. Alex is the champion.

06–07 Skeleton
1. Paramonovo is longer (1.60 km) than
Igls (1.22 km).
2. a) Calgary is the longest.
b) Whistler has the longer
vertical drop.
c) Whistler has more curves.
3. Alterberg (1.413 km), Winterberg
(1.330 km), Konigssee (1.306 km),
Oberhof (1.069 km)
4. a) Sochi (1.814 km)
b) Whistler (152 m)
c) Lake Placid (20 curves)

08–09 Hang gliding
1. 28:4 = 7:1 18:6 = 3:1 27:3 = 9:1
2. 72:8 = 9:1 so the right-hand triangle
has the same glide ratio.
3. a) 35:5 = 7:1 b) 15:2 = 7.5:1
c) 113:10 = 11.3:1
d) 41:4 = 10.25:1
4. Glide path c) is the most
impressive with a ratio
of 11.3:1

10–11 Windsurfing
1. Between 7 m² and 8 m² would be a good
estimate.
2. a) 3 m² b) 4.9 m² c) 6.7 m²
3. a) 8.6 m² b) 4.6 m² c) 3.2 m²
4. Lucy and Clive

12–13 Ice climbing
1. a) 65°, b) 90°, c) 85°, d) 105°
2. a) 7 cm b) 5 cm   c) 6 cm   d) 5 cm
3. a) 7 x 100 = 700 cm = 7 m
b) 5 x 800 = 4000 cm = 40 m
c) 6 x 600 = 3600 cm = 36 m
d) 5 x 1000 = 5000 cm = 50 m
4. A, C, B, D

14–15 Mogul skiing
1. a) (50% of 30) + (25% of 20) +
(25% of 12) = 23
b) (60% of 30) + (20% of 20) +
(20% of 12) = 24.4
2. The second competition
3. a) (50% of 20) + (25% of 28) +
(25% of 13) = 20.25
b) (60% of 20) + (20% of 28) +
(20% of 13) = 20.2
4. The first competition

16–17 Motocross

1. a) 40.6 – 35.5 = 5.1 cm
   b) 53.2 – 49.0 = 4.2 cm
2. a) 3.14 x 53.2 = 167 cm
   b) 3.14 x 49.0 = 153.9 cm
3. a) 10 x 1.672 = 16.72 m
   b) 10 x 1.54 = 15.4 m
4. a) 585.2 ÷ 1.672 = 350
   b) 585.2 ÷ 1.54 = 380

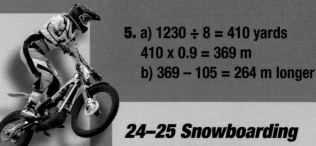

18–19 Caving

1. (-1, 5)
2. a) cathedral b) great chamber
   c) tube d) nose e) abyss
3. You would be at point (2, -2)
   in the part called 'cavern'.
4. Answers will vary, but can go left 2, up 1,
   left 3, down 3, left 1, down 2, left 1.

20–21 Abseiling

1. a) tan (40) x 500 = 419.5 m
   b) tan (45) x 800 = 800.0 m
   c) tan (60) x 900 = 1558.8 m
   d) tan (35) x 600 = 420.1 m
2. A and D
3. Both the distance from the base and the
   height are the same. This is because the
   triangle is an isosceles triangle with
   angles 45°, 45° and 90°.
4. a) C is the largest at 1558.8 m
   b) A is the smallest at 419.5 m

22–23 Slacklining

1. a) 2000 ft b) 2000 x 30 = 60,000 cm
   c) 60,000 ÷ 100 = 600 m
2. a) 23,000 cm b) 23,000 ÷ 100 = 230 m
   c) 230 ÷ 1000 = 0.23 km
3. 1.2 km = 1200 m 1200 – 185 = 1015 m
4. 363 x 0.9 = 326.7 m

5. a) 1230 ÷ 8 = 410 yards
   410 x 0.9 = 369 m
   b) 369 – 105 = 264 m longer

24–25 Snowboarding

1. Zhang Shi = 296
    Ivan Plotchedov = 347
    David Jenner = 362
    Amru Szalji = 352
    Andreas Shultz = 379
    Kyle Robertson = 386
2. Zhang Shi = 296 ÷ 4 = 74
    Ivan Plotchedov = 347 ÷ 4 = 86.75
    David Jenner = 362 ÷ 4 = 90.50
    Amru Szalji = 352 ÷ 4 = 88.00
    Andreas Shultz = 379 ÷ 4 = 94.75
    Kyle Robertson = 386 ÷ 4 = 96.50
3. Kyle Robertson 96.50
    Andreas Schultz 94.75
    David Jenner 90.50
    Amru Szalji 88.00
    Ivan Plotchedov 86.75
    Zhang Shi 74
4. a) Kyle Robertson
   b) Andreas Schultz
   c) David Jenner

26–27 Wakeboarding

1. 20 ÷ 5 = 4   4 x 8 = 32 km/h
2. 40 ÷ 8 = 5   5 x 5 = 25 mph
3. a) one quarter turn
   b) four quarter turns
4. a) two half turns
   b) three half turns
   c) four half turns
5. a) 540 ÷ 360 = 1½
   b) 720 ÷ 360 = 2
   c) 900 divided by 360 = 2½
   d) 1080 divided by 360 = 3

MATHS GLOSSARY

ACUTE ANGLE
An angle that is less than 90°.

ANGLE
The amount of turn, measured in degrees (°). There are 360 degrees in one full turn.

AREA
The amount of two-dimensional space covered by a shape or object. For example, the area of a rectangle is calculated by multiplying the length of one of the short sides by the length of one of the long sides.

CIRCUMFERENCE
The perimeter of a circle, the distance all the way around its edge.

DECIMAL
A number with a decimal point in it. The digit to the left of the decimal point is the number of units, while the digit to the right is the number of tenths.

DIAMETER
The widest length across a circle, passing through the centre.

FORMULA
A system of numbers, symbols and letters that is used to describe a mathematical relationship. Its plural is formulae.

KNOT
The speed when travelling at 1 nautical mile per hour.

MEAN AVERAGE
The average found by adding all the values and dividing by the number of values there are.

MEDIAN
The middle value of a set of values arranged in order of size.

MODE
The most popular or common value in a set of values.

MULTIPLE
The result of multiplying one number by another number.

NEGATIVE NUMBER
These are numbers on the other side of zero from positive numbers. We write them using the minus sign (-), e.g. -5, -3, -7.

OBTUSE ANGLE
An angle that is between 90° and 180°.

PERCENTAGE
A percentage is a fraction with a denominator of 100, e.g. 42% = $^{42}/_{100}$. Per cent means 'for every hundred'.

PERIMETER
The total distance around a shape. It is calculated by adding together the lengths of all the shape's sides.

PI
Written as π, pi is a special number that is approximately 3.1412 or $^{22}/_{7}$. It is the relationship between the diameter and circumference of a circle.

PROTRACTOR
A mathematical instrument, shaped in a circle or a semi-circle. It is marked with degrees and used to measure angles.

QUADRANT
One of the four sections created when a shape is divided by two lines that cross, such as the x-axis and y-axis.

RADIUS
The distance between the centre of a circle and its circumference.

RATIO
Ratios show how one or more numbers or values are related to another. So a ratio of 2:1 shows that there are twice as many of the first value as there are of the second.

RIGHT-ANGLED TRIANGLE
A triangle that has a right angle, 90°, as one of its angles.

SCALE
A number that shows how much a map or drawing has been made smaller. For example, a scale of 1:100 means that the drawing is 100 times smaller than the original, so 1 cm on the drawing represents 100 cm, or 1 m, in real life.

TAN OR TANGENT
The tangent of an angle in a right-angled triangle is the relationship between the opposite side to the angle divided by the adjacent side (not the longest side, the hypotenuse).

31

WEIGHTED SCORE
A total score made by combining different scores, where some of the scores are more important than others.

INDEX

32

WEBSITES

www.mathisfun.com
A huge website packed full of explanations, examples, games, puzzles, activities, worksheets and teacher resources for all age levels.

www.bbc.co.uk/bitesize
The revision section of the BBC website, it contains tips and easy-to-follow instructions on all subjects, including maths, as well as games and activities.

www.mathplayground.com
An action-packed website with maths games, mathematical word problems, worksheets, puzzles and videos.

ACKNOWLEDGEMENTS

Published in paperback in
Great Britain
in 2018 by Wayland

Copyright © Hodder and
Stoughton, 2016

All rights reserved
Editor: Elizabeth Brent

Produced by Tall Tree Ltd
Editors: Joe Fullman and
Rob Colson
Designer: Ed Simkins

ISBN: 978 0 7502 9848 3

Wayland, an imprint of Hachette Children's Group
Part of Hodder and Stoughton
Carmelite House
50 Victoria Embankment
London EC4Y 0DZ

An Hachette UK Company
www.hachette.co.uk
www.hachettechildrens.co.uk

Printed and bound in China

10 9 8 7 6 5 4 3 2 1

The website addresses (URLs) included in this book
were valid at the time of going to press. However, it is
possible that contents or addresses may have changed
since the publication of this book. No responsibility for
any such changes can be accepted by either the
author or the Publisher.

Picture credits
4-5 istockphoto.com/MichaelSvoboda, 6 istockphoto.com/
Sabonis, 8 istockphoto.com/ DCorn, 9 istockphoto.com/Andrzej
Burak, 10-11 istockphoto.com/LifeJourneys, 12-13
istockphoto.com/vm, 14-15 istockphoto.com/raclro, 16t
istockphoto.com/MarcelC, 17t istockphoto.com/ZagE, 17b
istockphoto.com/GibsonPictures, 18t and 19br istockphoto.
com/Eduard Andras, 19t Dreamstime.com/Salajean, 20-21
istockphoto.com/gregepperson, 23 istockphoto.com/
JaredAlden, 25 istockphoto.com/Jason Lugo, 26 istockphoto.
com/4x6, 26-27 istockphoto.com/KeithBinns

MIX
Paper from
responsible sources
FSC® C104740